D0988734

WISHES

SENIOR AUTHORS
Virginia A. Arnold
Carl B. Smith

LITERATURE CONSULTANTS
Joan I. Glazer
Margaret H. Lippert

Macmillan Publishing Company
New York

Collier Macmillan Publishers
London

ACKNOWLEDGMENTS

The publisher gratefully acknowledges permission to reprint the following copyrighted material:

"Glad to Have a Friend Like You" by Carol Hall is from FREE TO BE YOU AND ME. Copyright © 1972 Free To Be Foundation, Inc. and reprinted with their permission.

"I Dance in My Red Pajamas" is abridged and adapted from I DANCE IN MY RED PAJAMAS by Edith Thatcher Hurd. Copyright © 1982 by Edith Thatcher Hurd. By permission of Harper & Row, Publishers, Inc.

"Not Scared" from THE ZOO THAT GREW by Ilo Orleans. Reprinted by permission of Karen S. Solomon.

"The Question" from DOGS & DRAGONS, TREES & DREAMS: A Collection of Poems by Karla Kuskin. Copyright © 1958 by Karla Kuskin. By permission of Harper & Row, Publishers, Inc.

"Until We Built A Cabin" from THAT'S WHY by Aileen Fisher. Published by Thomas Nelson & Sons, New York, 1946. Copyright renewed 1974 by Aileen Fisher. Reprinted by permission of the author.

Cover Design: Bass and Goldman Associates

Illustration Credits: Olive Albert, 22–29; Don Almquist, 184–195; Sheryl Arneman, 196–200, 203–204; Karen Baumen, 140–151; Bob Brown, 218–227; Judith Cheng, 86–96; Dee DeRosa, 32–43; Lulu Delacre, 97; Susan Dodge, 20–21, 52–53, 76, 98–99, 154, 156; Marla Frazee, 110–119; Ponder Gombel, 175; Jon Goodell, 207; Gay Holland, 100–107; Tom Huffman, 78–85, 108–109; Marilyn Janovitz, 68–75; Bob LoGrippo, 152–153; Jimmy Longacre, 60–64, 66; Verlin Miller, 229–238; Sal Murdocca, 44–51, 164–169, 171–172, 174; Bob Shein, 30–31; Jerry Smath, 128–138; Lorna Tomei, 209–217; Lane Yerkes, 10–12, 14–16, 18–19.

Cover Photo: © Suzanne Szasz

Photo Credits: © Clara Aich, 22–23, 81–84. © George Ancona, 108. Barbara Kirk, 178L & R, 179–180, 180 inset, 181, 182T & B. © Harold M. Lambert Studios, Inc., 26–27. © Lawrence Migdale, 54, 56–58, 121–126. Photo Researchers, Inc.: © Soames Summerhays, 26. Photo Trends: © Victoria Beller Smith, 24. The Stock Market: © Robert Neumann, 25. © Suzanne Szasz, 8, 157–163.

Macmillan Publishing Company
866 Third Avenue
New York, N.Y. 10022
Collier Macmillan Canada, Inc.

Printed in the United States of America

ISBN 0–02–160060–0

9 8 7 6 5 4 3 2

Contents

5

UNIT ONE LEVEL 6

ON MY OWN

PREPARING FOR READING

Learning Vocabulary

Listen.

<u>s</u>top

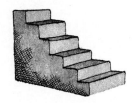  

Read.

1. The boy and girl like to go to the <u>store</u>.
2. You can get a book or a game <u>there</u>.
3. The boy likes <u>his</u> game.
4. The girl likes <u>her</u> book.
5. What will they get the <u>next</u> time they go to the store?

store   there   his   her   next

Developing Background

Read and talk.

Grandma's Store

Grandma runs a store. Jenny helps her. At the store you can get a ball or a bat. There are paints and pictures, too. Do you have a pet? Grandma can show you a book on a hamster or a kitten. Jenny can show you a game or some shells. You can get something that you will like at Grandma's store.

SOMETHING FOR PIP

Judith Davis

Jenny liked to help Grandma run her store. Each time Jenny came, there was something for her to do. This time, Grandma asked her to help the children who came into the store.

Jenny spoke to the next boy who walked in. "May I help you?" she asked. "What are you looking for?"

"Something little, for a friend," he said.

"Did you see this little submarine?" asked Jenny. "You should see it dive under the water. It can go very fast."

"My friend does not like water," said the boy.

"Take a look at this little plane," said Jenny. "It can fly for a long time."

"He does not like to fly," said the boy.

"Your friend should like this car," said Jenny. "It does not take long to make it."

"It is *too* little," said the boy.

"Your friend should pick what he likes," said Jenny. "Where is he?"

"He is in his house," said the boy. He put a little box down next to Jenny. Very slowly, a little brown hamster came out of the box. "This is my friend Pip. I am Ben."

"Very happy to see you both," said Jenny. "I am Jenny. What can I show you, Pip?" Then Jenny said to Ben, "Why don't I show you a . . ."

WHOOSH! What looked like a huge black ball flew at Pip.

"Look out, Pip!" said Ben. "Look out for the cat!"

"Stop!" Jenny said to the big black cat.

The cat didn't stop. The little hamster didn't have much time to run, but he was very fast. It didn't take long for Pip to hide next to some paints.

"Come to me," Jenny said to the cat. "You must go out now." She put the cat out of the store.

"Where did Pip go?" asked Ben.

"Look next to the paints," said Jenny. Pip was not there. "Look next to that ball and bat," said Jenny.

"I did," said Ben. "He is not there. Pip is not in the store."

"He will show up," said Jenny.

"You should have said there was a cat in the store," said Ben.

"You should have said your friend was a hamster," said Jenny. Then she asked, "What does Pip like to do at home?"

"He likes to eat," said Ben.

"I will put something out for Pip to eat," said Jenny. "He should come out then." But Pip did not come out.

"Where does Pip hide at home when something is scary?" asked Jenny.

"He runs into something little, like his box," said Ben. He put the box out for Pip, but the hamster didn't come out. "What will Pip do at night?" asked Ben. "It will get cold and scary."

"What does Pip like to do at night, when he is home with you?" asked Jenny.

"He likes to sit on my foot when I read a book," said Ben.

"I have it!" said Jenny. "There is a little book in the store for you and Pip. Read it now, and see what Pip does."

Jenny asked Grandma to help her make it look like night in the store. They did. It was very quiet in the store. Ben looked at the little book. This is what he read:

Make a Home for Your Pet

Does your hamster like to hide in something little? You can make a little house that it will like very much.

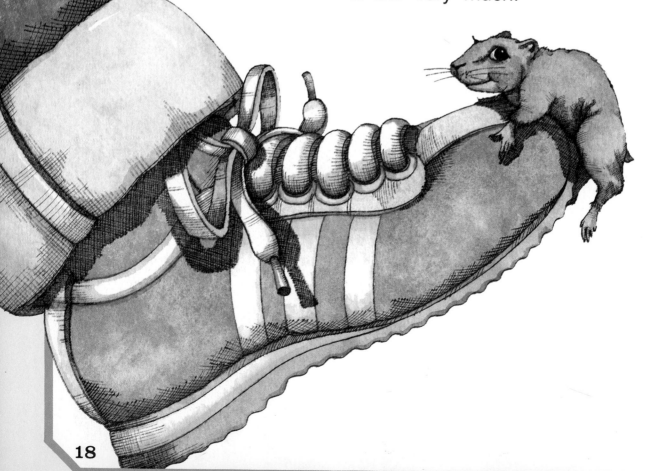

Very slowly, a little brown hamster came up to Ben. With a jump and a slide, it was up on his foot. It was Pip.

"Look at that," said Jenny. "A hamster that likes to read!"

"Pip, you funny little hamster," said Ben. "Look what I have for you! *This* is the little something I was looking for."

Questions

Read and think.
1. What did Ben have in his little box?
2. Why did Pip run and hide?
3. What did Ben do to make Pip come out?

PREPARING FOR READING

Learning Vocabulary

Listen.

spots

Read.

1. The school will have a <u>special</u> show in May.
2. The running <u>team</u> will be in a <u>race</u>.
3. Some boys and girls will do a special <u>dance</u>.

special   team   race   dance

Developing Background

Read and talk.

The Hobby Show

People like to come to the hobby show at my school. A hobby is something special that you like to do. A boy likes to race little cars. A man paints pictures for his hobby. A girl takes pictures. At a hobby show, you can pick a hobby you may like to do.

TIME FOR A HOBBY

Patricia Hinds

There is a time to work and a time to play. Some people take time to do something special. A hobby is something special for them. A hobby is something you do because you like it.

A hobby can be for one boy or girl. Or, a team of children can work on a hobby.

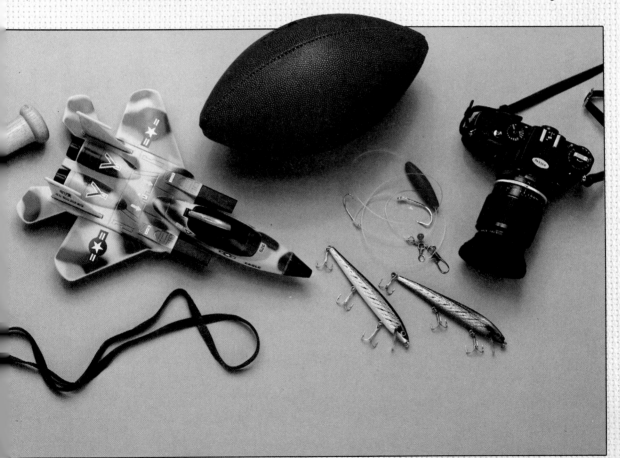

This is a hobby for one. The girl likes to dance. She can dance each day when school is out.

This hobby is for a team. The
children on the team like to play ball.
They play in the park when they can.

Some people like a quiet hobby. This
boy likes to go fishing with his father.
They go out on the water in a little boat.
When they get a fish, they are very
happy. Fishing can be a quiet hobby.

Some people have a hobby that is not so quiet. The children in this park like to race cars. First, each one must make a car. They may get help to do that. Then one day they go to the park to race the cars. The one who is first will get something special to take home!

Some people like to read for a hobby. Some people like to write. Some people like to paint pictures. This woman likes the woods. She is looking for a special bird. She will take pictures of the bird.

When you grow up, what hobby will you have? You may race cars or fly a plane. You may play on a team or go to see a team play at the ball park. Your hobby will be something you like. Your hobby will be special to you.

Pick a hobby you like. Do it when you have the time. Read or run, play or dance. A hobby can make you very happy. It can last for a long time.

Questions

Read and think.
1. What is a hobby?
2. What hobby can be for a team?
3. What can you do when you like a quiet hobby?
4. What hobby do you like to do?

FISHING

When I go fishing
I'm always wishing
Some fish will be my prize;
But while I'm fishing
The fish are wishing
  Otherwise.

And all the wishes
Of all the fishes
Seem always to come true;
So all my wishes
To catch some fishes
　Never do.

Unknown

31

PREPARING FOR READING

Learning Vocabulary

Listen.

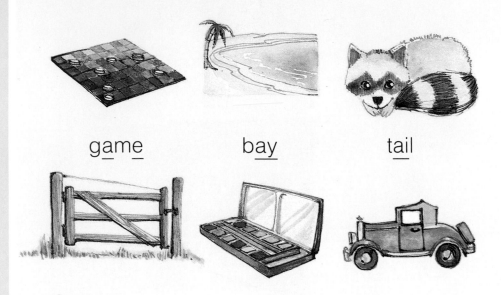

game   bay   tail

Read.

1. I <u>gave</u> some <u>rocks</u> to my friend.
2. She will make a <u>collection</u> of rocks.
3. Her collection of <u>stickers</u> was picked to be in the hobby show.
4. Both she and I are in a collection <u>club</u> at school.

gave   rocks   collection
stickers   club

Developing Background

Read and talk.

The Shell Collection

I am Katie. I have a shell collection. To make my collection, I look for the shells that are special. I put them in a box. Then I have a book in which I write what each shell is and what it looks like. A shell collection does take time, but I like it.

The Collection Club

Gibbs Davis

"Have you seen my shell collection?" Katie asked Jeff one day at school. She gave Jeff one of the shells in her box. "I am in the collection club."

"What is a collection club?" asked Jeff. "What do you do there?"

"Come to the club with me," Katie said. "You will see."

At the collection club, the teacher said to Jeff, "The collection club is a special hobby for each boy and girl. First you make a collection of something you like. Then you show it to the club."

"You must have a collection to get into the club," Katie said to Jeff.

"What is your collection, Jeff?" asked the teacher. Jeff looked at Pam's book of stickers and Ted's little cars.

"Pets!" he said.

"Pets," said Pam, "What is a collection of pets?"

"When can we see it?" asked Ted.

"Next time," said Jeff.

"We will be happy to see your collection next time," the teacher said. "Now it is time to go home."

Katie and Jeff walked home. "When I was at your house I didn't see pets," Katie said. "What do you have? A dog? A cat? Some fish?"

Jeff was very quiet. It was true. He didn't have a pet. Not one.

"Look!" Katie said. She picked up three pretty rocks. She gave them to Jeff. "They look like bird eggs," she said.

"They are not bird eggs. They are rocks," said Jeff. "I don't have time to play now. I have to work on my collection. See you."

"May I get some pets for my collection?" Jeff asked his mother.

"Pets eat too much and they jump on people," she said. "Grandma gave you some cute little stickers. Why not make a collection of stickers?"

"I don't like stickers," said Jeff. "May I go for a walk?"

"You may," said his mother, "but don't go where I can't see you."

Jeff walked slowly out of the house. He looked for fish in the water. There were some red and green rocks. One looked like a fish. Jeff spoke to it. "I wish you were a live fish," he said. "I wish you were in my pet fish collection." He picked up the rocks.

Then Jeff looked for pets in the
woods. He was not happy. He didn't
have one pet to show the next day at
the collection club. He looked down at
some rocks. He let them slide under his
foot. He picked them up and walked
slowly home. Jeff didn't have much hope.

"Where is your collection, Jeff?"
asked the teacher the next day. Jeff
didn't have one, but he couldn't say it.
Katie looked sad for her friend.

Jeff jumped up to go. Then rocks
came falling down on Jeff's foot.

"Look!" Katie said. "A collection of rocks!" Jeff looked down at the rocks. It was true. The rocks did make a collection.

"But where are your pets?" asked a boy.

Jeff looked to Katie for help. "You are looking at Jeff's pets," she said. "This is Jeff's collection of pet rocks."

"You have a very special collection," said the teacher.

"I have a very special friend," said Jeff.

Questions

Read and think.
1. What was Katie's collection?
2. What did Jeff say was in his collection?
3. What was Jeff's very special collection?

PREPARING FOR READING

Learning Vocabulary

Listen.

a <u>small</u> bird

Read.

1. The bird flew to a <u>small</u> <u>tree</u>.

2. "I must have a <u>drink</u> because I am <u>thirsty</u>," said the bird.

3. Down <u>by</u> the small tree, the bird saw something.

4. There was a <u>pitcher</u> of water.

small tree drink
thirsty by   pitcher

Developing Background
Read and talk.

A Special Pet

A crow is a big, black bird. I have a friend in the country with a pet crow. He says his crow likes to play a trick now and then. When something is missing, he looks for his pet. The crow will take something like a shell and hide it. One time the crow flew up in a tree with some rope.

My friend says that you could call his crow a "collection crow." Why does he say that?

45

THE
CROW
AND THE
PITCHER

retold by Margaret H. Lippert

A thirsty crow flew to a big tree. He was looking for water to drink. There was a pitcher under the tree, so he flew down to the pitcher. He looked into it. There was a little water in the pitcher.

The crow said, "I am thirsty. I will drink the water in this pitcher." But the crow couldn't drink the water. The top of the pitcher was too small. He couldn't get down to the water, so he couldn't have a drink.

"I am so thirsty," the crow said. "I must have a drink. I must get that water." The crow flew to a big rock by the tree. He said, "I can't get down to the water because the top of the pitcher is too small. I have to get the water up to the top of the pitcher. Then I can sit on the top of the pitcher and drink."

There were some small rocks by the big rock. The crow said, "I can pick up some small rocks and put the rocks into the pitcher. Then the water will get up to the top of the pitcher, and I can drink. That will do the trick."

The crow put a small rock into the pitcher. The water came up a little. He flew to get the next small rock, and he put that one into the pitcher. One by one, he put small rocks into the pitcher. Little by little, the water came up and up.

At last, the water came up to the top of the pitcher, so the thirsty crow could drink.

Then the crow flew to the top of the tree. He was happy. He said, "I did it! I could take a drink! Little by little does the trick."

Questions

Read and think.
1. Why couldn't the crow drink the water in the pitcher?
2. What did the crow do to get the water?
3. Why did the crow say, "Little by little does the trick"?

PREPARING FOR READING

Learning Vocabulary

Listen.

sneakers

Read.

1. I put on sneakers to play basketball.
2. When I can't make shots, I pass the ball to my friend.
3. She runs down to the hoop.
4. Look at her make two points.

sneakers   shots   pass
hoop   points

Developing Background

Read and talk.

The Blue Sneakers

At my school we have a basketball team called the Blue Sneakers. We play with a special hoop. We pass and dribble the ball. We run and jump to make shots for points. Each boy and girl on the Blue Sneakers team gets some time to play in each game.

BASKETBALL

NANCY WHISLER

Basketball is my hobby. Each day I fly out of school and rush home. I put on my sneakers.

Then I stop by and get my friend, Mike, at his house. Mike and I both have sneakers on. Mike says sneakers help you run and jump. We dribble the basketball when we go up the walk to the park.

It is so much work to have a top basketball team! First we walk a little, then we run. Running is a must, because it helps the team play a fast game.

Next we work on the pass. Each two people have a basketball. I play with Mike. He teaches me when to dribble the ball and when to pass it. This will help to make points.

Mike helps me work on my dribble. I do a fast dribble. Dribble and run, dribble and run. Mike runs under the hoop. "Dribble the ball. Then pass it to me," he calls. We work and work.

Dribble, run, dribble, run. Then I pass it to Mike. He can jump up and put it in.

BASKETBALL

To make points in basketball, you must get the ball in the hoop. Mike and I work on shots. He teaches me to jump up when I have the ball under the hoop. This helps me get the ball up next to the hoop. Then I can put it in and make two points.

BASKETBALL

58

Long shots have to go into the hoop, too. Some of my long shots are missing the hoop. To play top basketball, I have to work on my long shots.

I like it when we play a game. Each team will make some points. People on each team dribble and pass. They run and jump. What a game we have! I am happy that I get to play basketball each day in the park. It is work, but it is play, too.

Questions

Read and think.
1. What does the boy like to do each day when school gets out?
2. Why is running a must in basketball?
3. Why does the boy have to work on his long shots?

PREPARING FOR READING

Learning Vocabulary

Listen.

dive   fly   night

Read.

1. Dribble to the <u>right</u> and then jump.
2. Now <u>turn</u> and pass to the <u>left</u>.
3. Dribble <u>around</u> the players to the hoop.
4. Now turn <u>away</u> and jump up to the hoop.

right   turn   left   around   away

Developing Background

Read and talk.

A Team

Do you like to play on a team? You may be right for a ball team or a running team. To be on a team, you should like to do what the team does. Do you have the time to be on a team? Do you like to work? It will take time and work to be on a team.

In *Elena Can Do It*, Elena likes to play basketball. Will she be on the team?

Elena CAN Do It!

Nancy Whisler

Each day when she left school, Elena liked to stop and see the basketball team play.

"Why don't you play basketball, Elena?" asked her father one day. "I have seen you jump. You can be on the team. Why don't you see Mr. King?"

"I can't be on the team," said Elena. "I can't run fast."

The next day, Mr. King spoke to Elena. "My team came in last in the city basketball club, Elena," he said. "My players can run fast and dribble the ball. They can pass to the left and to the right. They can turn and run with the ball. But they can't get it into the hoop!"

Elena looked at the team play. She could see that Mr. King was right. The players could turn around fast to the left. They could turn around fast to the right. But they couldn't make points.

At last Elena spoke up. "I may be a help to the team, Mr. King," she said.

"You, Elena?" asked Mr. King.

"I can do it," said Elena.

"Why not?" said Mr. King. "You have your sneakers on. Get in there!"

It was scary for Elena to go into the game. But she couldn't turn away now. The players looked at Elena. Right away, one boy called out, "Elena can't play. Basketball players have to run fast. She's not fast."

Elena looked around at the players. She was very red. "He is right," she said. "I can't run very fast, but you can't make points. I can make shots. Shots make points. I can help you."

"Come on, team!" called Mr. King.

Did that team play! Dribble, run, pass! Dribble, run, pass! At last a pass came to Elena. She was the one to jump and put the ball right into the hoop.

"Hurray!" said Elena.

"Hurray!" said the players. "She didn't jump. She *flew* into the air!"

"You are on the team, Elena," said Mr. King. "Some players run fast, and some pass the ball. But you will make shots. We will run away with the next game! With your help we will be the top team now!"

Questions

Read and think.

1. Why did Mr. King's team come in last in the city basketball club?
2. What did one boy say when Elena came into the game?
3. What did Elena do with the pass?

PREPARING FOR READING

Learning Vocabulary

Listen.

dive   fly   night

Read.

1. I <u>might</u> like to be in a circus.
2. I could play <u>music</u> and my bear could dance.
3. People will <u>smile</u> at my bear and me.
4. It looks <u>strange</u> to see a bear dance.
5. When I <u>lost</u> my bear, I couldn't be in the circus.

might   music   smile   strange   lost

Read and talk.

A Music Box

A music box can make you smile. It can play happy music or sad music. It can be little or big. It might have a lion or a dog on top of it. The dog or lion will turn around in time to the music.

In *The Music Box Bear*, Amanda and her father have a special music box. Why is it so special?

The Music Box Bear

Carol Carrick

Amanda liked bears. She liked to have bears around her. She liked to make pictures of bears. She liked her collection of bears.

"Bears, bears, bears," said her father.

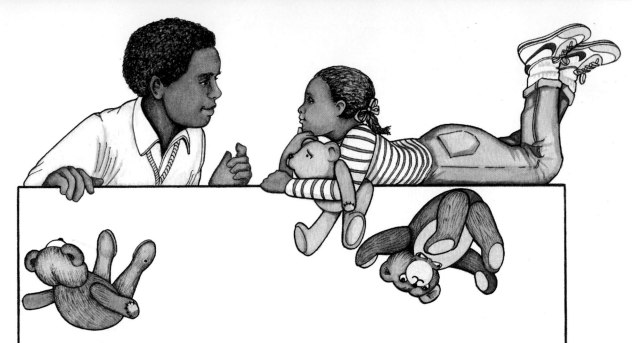

"You have a hobby," Amanda said to her father. Each night, you sit and work on a music box. I have a hobby, too. I have a bear collection. Bears make me smile."

"You might like to see a live bear," said Amanda's father. "A special circus is in the city. We will go to see it."

The next night Amanda and her father were at the circus. "What a big tent!" said Amanda.

"It is called the Big Top," said her father.

A man called out, "See the little dog drive a truck! See the lion jump in and out of a hoop! See the bear dance!"

"Where is the bear?" asked Amanda.

"Right there," said her father.

Amanda was so happy. The bear could do a trick. It could dance when the music played. It turned around and around.

"It is strange to see a bear dance," said Amanda. "It looks like a music box."

"It does!" said her father with a smile.

Amanda and her father left the circus tent. "Play the hoop game!" called a woman. "Get a bear like the one under the Big Top!"

"I might get a bear!" said Amanda. "What do I have to do?"

"To make points, you must get the hoop around one of the red spots," the woman said. "Make three points and you get a bear." Amanda played and played, but she lost each time.

"I might do it," said her father, but he lost, too.

"I have a bear at home," Amanda said with a smile.

The next day, one of Amanda's bears was missing. "This is very strange," she said.

"What is strange?" asked her father.

"My little brown bear is lost," said Amanda.

"It will turn up," said her father.

"I hope so," said Amanda.

That night her father said, "Look what turned up."

"My bear!" said Amanda.

"Now it is a music box," said her father. "And it is for you."

"It looks like the bear at the circus!" said Amanda. "Did you make it for me? Why?"

"Because you are very special to me," said her father. "Because you make me smile. And because you like bears so much."

The music played, and the little bear turned around and around.

Questions

Read and think.
1. What was Amanda's collection?
2. What could the bear in the circus do?
3. What did Amanda's father do with one of her bears?

WRITING ACTIVITY

WRITE A TIME-ORDER PARAGRAPH

Prewrite

Amanda liked the circus. There was so much for her to see there. Look at the pictures. They show what Amanda looked at in the circus.

1

2

3

4

What did Amanda see first?

Then what did Amanda see?

What did Amanda look at next?

What did she see last?

Write

1. Write your paragraph on what Amanda saw on your paper.

2. This can be your first sentence.

   Amanda liked to go to the circus.

3. Look at the pictures on page 76. Write sentences that say what Amanda looked at in the circus. Use words like *first*, *then*, *next*, and *last* in your sentences.

4. Use your Glossary for help with words.

Revise

Read your paragraph. Do your sentences say what Amanda looked at in the circus? Did you use words like *first*, *then*, *next*, and *last*?

Read with your teacher.

1. Do your sentences begin with capital letters?

2. Do your sentences end with periods?

PREPARING FOR READING

Learning Vocabulary

Listen.

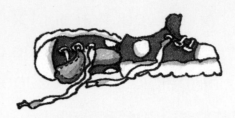

sneakers

Read.

1. You can <u>snap</u> things to make music.
2. You can <u>tap</u> things like <u>glasses</u>, too.
3. Look around your home for <u>things</u> you <u>need</u>.
4. You can make your <u>own</u> music.

snap   tap   glasses
things   need   own

Developing Background

Read and talk.

Where is Music?

My teacher likes music very much. He
says that strange things can make music.
The wind can make music. A calling bird can
make its own music. Things that tap and
snap make music, too. My teacher says to
put on your music glasses and look around.
Where is the music around you?

79

MAKE YOUR OWN MUSIC

Anne Rockwell

Do you like music? You can make your own music. You can make your own instrument to make music. You might have the things you need to make an instrument right in your house. Some funny things will make music. Look around you. What do you see that can make music?

Can glasses make music? They can when you put water in them. You will need some water glasses and a pitcher of water.

Look at this picture. Your water glasses should look like the picture. Now tap on the glasses. Do you like the music? You have an instrument to make your own music.

You can make music with nails, too. You
will need some nails. Look at this picture.
When your nails look like the picture, tap
them. You have an instrument to make
music. Don't funny things make music?

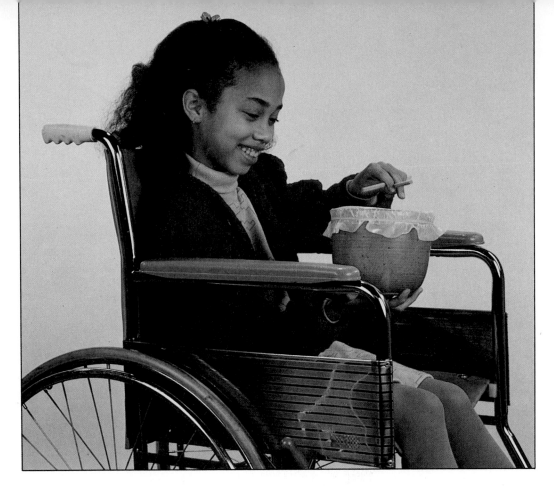

You can make your own drum. You
will need a box or a can. Look at the
picture. Make a drum like the one in the
picture. Tap your drum slowly or tap it
fast.

What things can you snap to make music? Look at the things in the picture that you can snap. Make your own instrument to snap. You can snap it slowly or very fast. You can snap this instrument in time with your drum.

Now get a friend or two to help you make music. Each friend must have one instrument. One friend can play the glasses, and one can play a drum. One can snap an instrument in time to the drum.

Make music slowly, or make it fast.
Make your music happy or sad, funny or
strange. It is your own special music.

Questions

Read and think.

1. What can you do with glasses that have water in them?
2. What do you need to make a drum?
3. What do you see around you that can make music?

PREPARING FOR READING

Learning Vocabulary

Listen.

dive   fly   night

Read.

1. See the girl kick her legs <u>high</u> in the air.

2. <u>Every</u> <u>step</u> in her dance must be right.

3. She does so <u>want</u> to be a dancer.

high   every   step   want

Developing Background

Read and talk.

Peter Pan

Peter Pan is a play. In the play, Peter Pan is a boy who does not want to grow up. Wendy is his friend. Peter Pan can fly, and he teaches Wendy and the other children in the play to fly, too. The children in the play do a dance called a ballet.

Melissa and Tami both want to be Wendy in the play. Who will be Wendy?

WHO WILL BE WENDY?

Barbara Greenberg

Melissa liked her friend Tami very much. When her blue sneakers came, she wanted Tami to be the first one to see them. She gave one of her two submarine stickers to Tami, because Tami was her friend. When Tami said that *The Bear Who Played Basketball* was a very funny book, Melissa read it, too.

Melissa liked to dance to music. At home she put on music so she could dance. She could turn and jump and kick in time to the music. She wanted to be a ballet dancer. Tami wanted to be a ballet dancer, too.

One day the ballet teacher said, "We will have a show. It will be *Peter Pan*. We will put on the show for two nights. I will pick children to be in it next time you come."

At home Melissa said to her mother, "Tami and I both want to be Wendy when we dance in *Peter Pan*. But there can't be two Wendys. The teacher might pick Tami and not me, and I will be sad."

Melissa's mother said, "The teacher may pick Tami. You will be sad at first, but you will not be sad for too long. The teacher may pick you. What will you do then?"

"Then Tami might not want to be my friend," said Melissa. "I want to be Wendy, and I don't want to be Wendy. What can I do?"

"Things will work out," said Melissa's mother. "You will see."

"I hope so," said Melissa.

When Tami and Melissa walked to school the next day, Melissa said to

Tami, "The teacher may pick you to be
Wendy and not me, but I will be your
friend."

"She might pick you," Tami said,
"but I will be your friend."

In school the teacher said, "I must pick children to be in the show. I will show you every step that I want you to do. First look at what I do. Next do each step with me. Then I want to see you do it."

The children looked at the teacher. She did a jump. They did one with her. Then the teacher turned around to see the children do the step. She said, "Now jump up high, up to the sky." Every girl and boy wanted to jump very high for her to see.

Melissa wanted to be Wendy so much. She wanted the teacher to see her turn and kick and jump in time to the music. She wanted the teacher to pick her to play Wendy. Tami was her friend, but Melissa wanted to be Wendy very much.

The children did every step. At last the teacher said, "I will pick the children to be in the show now." First she picked a boy to be Peter. Next she picked the mother and father and the lost children. Then she picked the dog.

At last the teacher turned to Tami and Melissa. She said, "Tami, you jump so high that you look like you are flying. You will be Wendy." Tami looked at Melissa.

She was happy to be Wendy, but
she wanted Melissa to be happy, too.

Melissa gave Tami a sad little smile.
But then the teacher said, "Melissa, you
turned so fast it looked like the wind
blew you around. You will be Wendy,
too. Tami will dance Wendy in the show
the first night, and Melissa will be
Wendy the next night. We have two
nights, so we will have two Wendys."

Melissa and Tami jumped up and down. "Two nights, two Wendys, and two friends!" they said.

Questions

Read and think.

1. Who did both Tami and Melissa want to be in *Peter Pan*?
2. What did the children have to do to see who could be in the show?
3. Why did the teacher pick two Wendys?

Glad To Have A Friend Like You

Peg told Greg
She liked to make things out of chairs.
Greg told Peg
Sometimes he still hugged teddy bears.

So they sneaked in the living room
And piled all the pillows up
And made it a rocket ship
To fly in.
And the bears were their girls and boys
And they were the astronauts
Who lived on the moon
With one pet lion,
Singin'

Glad to have a friend like you,
Fair and fun and skippin' free
Glad to have a friend like you,
And glad to just be me.

Carol Hall

PREPARING FOR READING

Learning Vocabulary

Listen.

a <u>sc</u>ared girl

Read.

1. A <u>scared</u> <u>rabbit</u> sees a <u>fox</u> running right at it.

2. Fox called, "<u>Wait</u> for me!"

3. Then Crow <u>sang</u> for Fox.

4. Fox could <u>skip</u> and dance to the music.

scared   rabbit   fox
wait   sang   skip

Developing Background

Read and talk.

Dance

Do you like to dance? Some children like to dance to fast music. Some like to dance slowly. Some skip, kick, snap, and tap when they dance. They want every step to be right.

In *The Rabbit's Trick*, Fox can skip and dance to get the cheese. What will Rabbit do for her trick?

THE RABBIT'S TRICK

Margaret H. Lippert

Crow liked to eat. He liked apples
and eggs, but what he liked very, very
much was cheese. He was happy when
he could get cheese to eat. One day
Crow came to where there was some
yellow cheese. He picked the cheese up
and flew to a big tree.

Now Rabbit was under the tree at the time. Rabbit looked up at Crow with the cheese. Like the crow, Rabbit liked cheese very, very much. "May I have some of your yellow cheese?" Rabbit asked. Crow did not want Rabbit to have his cheese, so Crow flew to the very top of the tree with the cheese.

Rabbit was sad because she wanted some of Crow's cheese. Rabbit didn't have time to be sad for long, because there was Fox running out of the woods. Fox was running right at her. Rabbit was scared. WHOOSH! Rabbit jumped and rushed away.

Now what Fox liked very, very much to eat was rabbit. "I will play a trick on Rabbit," he said. Fox called, "WAIT! Don't be scared. Wait for me!" But Rabbit did not wait. She jumped away fast, right into her home under the rocks.

Fox looked around. He wanted something to eat. He looked up in the tree, and there was Crow with the yellow cheese. Now Fox wanted that cheese. "I will have to trick Crow to get the cheese," he said.

"My friend," Fox called up to Crow,
"I like your music so much. Last night
when you sang I wanted to dance, so I
danced and danced. I like to dance when
I am happy, and I am happy now. I am
happy because I scared little Rabbit away.
I want to skip fast and jump high and
dance for a long time. Look at me skip
and jump and dance. Make music for me."

Crow wanted to see Fox skip and
jump and dance. He was happy that Fox
liked his music so much, so Crow sang.
When Crow sang, he let the cheese go.

Fox picked up the cheese and walked
away to eat it on the rocks by Rabbit's
house. Then Fox turned around and
called to Crow, "Look out for friends
who want what you have. They are not
true friends." Crow looked very, very sad.

Now Rabbit was looking out of her house at the time. She couldn't wait to play a trick on that fox. When Fox turned around and called to Crow, he let go of the cheese. Then Rabbit rushed out of her house.

WHOOSH! SNAP! Rabbit picked up the cheese and jumped right into her home. Fox looked around in time to see Rabbit's tail go into her house.

"WAIT!" he called. "That is my cheese." But Rabbit sang in her house.

"I have the cheese,
you don't, you see.
You can trick Crow,
but you can't trick me."

So both Fox and Crow lost the cheese.

Questions

Read and think.

1. What did Crow, Rabbit, and Fox like to eat?
2. Why did Crow fly away when Rabbit asked for the cheese?
3. Who played a trick on Crow to get the cheese?
4. Who had the cheese at last?

UNIT TWO LEVEL 6

ALL
TOGETHER

PREPARING FOR READING

Learning Vocabulary

Listen.

rope   crow   boat

Read.

1. I <u>know</u> I can't swim.

2. My <u>brother</u> says I should <u>try</u>.

3. <u>Swimming</u> is something he can teach me.

know   brother   try   swimming

Developing Background

Read and talk.

Are You Scared?

To be scared of something is not funny. Some people are scared of flying in a plane. Some don't like a big dog. Some people are scared to go out at night. Get help when you are scared. Your mother, father, or teacher will help you.

In *One Step at a Time*, Jennifer is scared of something. Her brother Bobby helps her. What does Bobby do for Jennifer?

ONE
STEP
AT A
TIME

Susan Alberghini

Jennifer and her brother Bobby were by the water. Jennifer looked at her friends. She could see them dive into the water and then kick and swim.

"Don't sit out there, Jennifer," called her friends. "Come on in! Try the water!"

"I can't!" called Jennifer.

"Why not?" her friends called. "Your brother is with you! He can see you swim!"

"I don't want to go in the water!" called Jennifer. "It is too cold! And I have to get some shells for my collection. I want to take some pictures for my Grandpa, too!"

113

"You don't need shells, Jennifer,"
said her brother. "You don't need to take
the pictures for Grandpa right now. I
know why you will not play in the
water. You can't swim. The water is
scary to you because you can't swim. I
know you want to play with your
friends, but you are scared of the water."

"You are right, Bobby," said Jennifer. "I want to swim, but I am too scared."

"I will help you," said Bobby. "I will be your swimming teacher. One day, you will jump and kick and dive. We will go slowly. We will take one step at a time. I know you can do it, but you must try."

At first Jennifer liked to go into the
water very slowly.

"The water is too cold," she said.

"You have to get under the water," said her brother. "Look at me." Bobby blew bubbles under the water. Then he came up. "Try that," he said.

Jennifer blew bubbles under the water. "That is funny," she said. "I like to do that. Do you know what, Bobby? Because of you, I might like swimming!"

"We can't go too fast," said Bobby. "We must take one step at a time. It will not be long, and you will be swimming. I know you will like it!"

Bobby and Jennifer did take one step at a time. One day Bobby said, "Now kick, Jennifer! Kick each foot fast, and you will go on top of the water." Jennifer kicked and kicked, and then she was swimming. At last she was swimming! "I can swim!" she called. "I can swim!"

"Hurray!" said Bobby. "I asked you to try, Jennifer, and you did!"

"I am so happy!" said Jennifer. "I can go in the water with my friends. I can dive in and swim around and around. Bobby, you are a special brother, and you are a special teacher, too. You are a teacher who teaches one step at a time."

Questions

Read and think.

1. Why didn't Jennifer want to go in the water?
2. What did Bobby do to help Jennifer?
3. Why did Jennifer say Bobby was a special teacher?

PREPARING FOR READING

Learning Vocabulary

Listen.

some + thing = something
air + plane = airplane
in + to = into

Read.

1. The <u>coach</u> of the swimming team teaches <u>lifesaving</u>.

2. He teaches lifesaving at the <u>pool</u>.

3. In lifesaving, you must <u>keep</u> an <u>eye</u> on the people swimming in the pool.

coach   lifesaving   pool
keep   eye ·

Developing Background

Read and talk.

A Letter

May 6, 1988

Dear Jennifer,

   In your last letter, you said you were swimming now. I am on the swimming team. The coach teaches me to race. Some children on my team like to dive. Some can dance under water. That is pretty to see. We go to the pool each day to work with the coach. When you come to see me, you can go to the pool, too.

Your friend,
Paul

THE SWIMMING TEAM

Paul likes to go to the pool. He likes to take swimming with the coach every day.

This is a special day for Paul. He is happy because his mother and father are at the pool. They want to see what he does with the swimming coach. Paul sits with his friends next to the pool. The swimming coach is with them.

Paul and his friends are on the swimming team. The coach teaches them to dive in the water and swim fast. She can time them when they swim. She teaches them that they must keep an eye on the boy or girl next to them in the pool. The coach will help them see what they must do to be first in a race.

Paul and his friends must know what to do when people need help in the water. Each of the children must keep an eye on the coach when she teaches them the special points of lifesaving. She teaches them what they can do on land to help. They should not go into the water for lifesaving, because they are too little. They must try to help on land. Paul and his friends each take a turn at lifesaving.

Paul's mother and father are happy they have seen Paul with his coach. They know the coach is special because the children like to work on swimming and lifesaving every day. They know the coach will keep an eye on Paul in the water. Now they can't wait to see the first race of the swimming team!

Questions

Read and think.

1. What does the swimming coach teach Paul?
2. What should Paul and his friends do when people need help in the water?
3. Why do Paul's mother and father know the coach is special?

PREPARING FOR READING

Learning Vocabulary

Listen.

rope   crow   boat

Read.

1. Do you like to <u>float</u> on the water?
2. The man <u>swam</u> because he didn't like to float.
3. Some birds <u>spread</u> <u>their</u> <u>wings</u> to float in the air.
4. They <u>move</u> their wings up and down when they fly.

float   swam   spread
their   wings   move

Developing Background

Read and talk.

A Home on a Boat

Some people like to make their home on a boat. First, people who live on a boat must like the water. Then, too, they must like a home that will float. With a home on the water, they can go fishing and swimming every day. When they want to move, they can move their home right away.

In *Three Friends*, Burly Bear, Charlene Chicken, and Fred Fox go to live on a boat. Will they like it?

THREE FRIENDS

Jerry Smath

Burly Bear wanted to move out of the big green woods. His friends Charlene Chicken and Fred Fox were sad. They did not want their friend to move away.

"Where will you live?" asked Fred Fox.

"I have a boat down on the bay," said Burly. "It will be my home. You know I like to fish. With a home on the water, I can fish and swim every day."

"We will miss you," said Charlene.

Burly said, "I know. I will miss you too, but . . . " Burly jumped up and looked at his friends. "Why don't you move on the boat with me?"

"I don't know," said Charlene. "I don't like the water very much."

Fred said, "We can try it."

So Burly Bear, Charlene Chicken, and
Fred Fox did move to the boat on the
bay. It was their home. Every day Burly
swam and swam and looked for fish.
Fred swam, but then he liked to float
on the water in the sun, too. Charlene
spread her wings and flew around the
boat. They sang and read. "What a team
we make!" Burly said. Every day was
special.

But then, little by little, things were not so special. One night the wind blew and blew. Their home was very scary then. The next day they could not see land. The sun did not come out. The sky looked strange. The water turned a funny green.

That day Burly said to his friends, "At first I liked to float around on my boat, but I don't want to float every day. I don't want to float in water like this. I miss my home in the green woods. I was happy in the woods, but I did not know it."

Fred missed his home, too. "I was happy in the woods," he said. "I like to run and hide in the woods. I can't run and hide on this small boat. At first I liked to float around on the boat. But now I want to go home."

Charlene didn't like to say so, but she missed her farm in the woods. "I like the boat," she said, "but it is a little too small. I can't move around much. Why don't we go home?"

"I know that we want to go home," said Burly, "but I can't see land. I don't know where we are."

"You don't know where we are!" said Charlene. She spread her wings and jumped up and down. "Why don't you know where we are? I am scared!"

"That is what I say," said Fred. "This is your boat. You should know where we are!"

Burly Bear said, "Now wait, friends. I will get the boat home, but we are a team. Will you help?"

"You are right," said Fred and Charlene. "We are a team. We will get home, scared or not. Now, what will we do first?"

Burly said, "First we must look for land. Charlene, you fly up in the sky and look."

Charlene spread her wings and flew up in the sky. "I see something green," she called. "It could be land."

Burly said, "Fred, look for rocks and things in the water. I will drive the boat."

So Charlene called down to Burly, "Go left," or "Go right." Fred looked for rocks, and Burly turned the boat in the water.

At long last the wind blew the boat
to land. The friends jumped out of the
boat. "At last," said Fred. "We are on
land."

"But what land are we on?" asked Charlene.

"I know," said Fred. "There are the big green woods."

Charlene said, "Look! I see my farm in the woods."

"Now I know where we are," said Burly Bear. He looked at Charlene and Fred. With a big smile he said, "We are home!"

Questions

Read and think.
1. Who were Burly Bear's friends?
2. Where did Burly and his friends move?
3. Why did Burly and his friends want to go home to the big green woods?

PREPARING FOR READING

Learning Vocabulary

Listen.

rope   crow   boat

Read.

1. The girl <u>drove</u> in her car to the country.
2. She wanted to see her <u>family</u>.
3. Her family moved to a <u>new</u> home in the country.

drove   family   new

Developing Background
Read and talk.

What is a Home?

A home is where you live. A home is where you can play with your friends. A home is where your family is. A home can be little or big. It can be in the city or the country. You can be happy or sad at home. Someday you may have to move out of your home. That may not be a happy time. Why?

141

THE CITY GIRL

Ada B. Litchfield

My family wanted to move, but I didn't. I didn't want to live in the country. I wanted to live in the city. I liked the city. The city was my home. I was a city girl.

"I know you don't want to go," said my father, "but I must work in the country now. We will live in a big house. You will like your new school, and you will make new friends. There are things that you will like. Wait and see."

My father wanted me to be happy, so I said, "I will try." But I didn't want to move.

"A truck will move the big things, but each of you can take something," said my mother.

"I will take my basketball," said Nan.

"I will take my paints," said Mark.

"I will take Eric," I said.

"I will take Bubbles," said Eric. Bubbles is Eric's pet fish. Eric is my little brother. He is too much.

First my father drove. Nan, Mark, Eric, and my mother sang. I was quiet.

Nan, Mark, Eric, and my mother looked for red cars. I didn't.

Then my mother drove. The family was quiet this time. My father wanted Eric to sleep, but he couldn't. "You know what?" Eric said to me. "In the country we can have a big pet. We can have a huge pet!"

"Like what?" I asked.

"Like an ostrich!" said Eric.

"An ostrich is not the right pet for this family, Eric," said my mother.

My mother drove on and on. At last we came to the country house. It was big, but it was not pretty. "That is not a new house!" I said.

"It is new to this family," said my mother.

"It looks scary," I said. "Bats could live there, but not people."

"People *will* live there," said my father. "It does need work, but we can do it. Each of you will help. We will work and work, and someday the house will look pretty."

"Do bats like fish?" asked Eric.

We moved into the house, and every day we did things to make it pretty. At last the house did look pretty, and my family was happy. My mother and father were happy, because they both like to do things around the house. Nan was happy, because she played basketball every day. Mark was happy, because he could have some quiet time to paint. Eric was happy, because he could play with Bubbles.

I was not happy. I didn't like the country. I missed the city.

One day Eric came up the walk with a friend. It was a big yellow dog. "Some family will be looking for that dog, Eric," I said. "It is their pet."

"I can't help it," said Eric. "I can't make it go away."

"It is a pretty dog," I said.

"Sit," said Eric, and the dog did.

That day Eric and I played with the dog. It could do a trick. It could dance on two legs. Eric said, "I will call the dog Blue, because the sky is so blue!"

"That is funny," I said, "because the dog is yellow!"

My father came out of the house. "You can't call it Blue or Yellow," he said, "because it can't be your pet. We will look for its family."

Eric was sad. So was I, but this time I didn't show it. "Someday we will get a big yellow dog, Eric," I said.

"That is true," said my father. "When we moved we said we could get a big pet. It is time for this family to have a dog."

"Can we get an ostrich, too?" asked Eric.

My father and I both said, "An ostrich is not the right pet for this family, Eric!"

That was the day when I liked the country for the first time. I looked at the big house, and I looked at the blue sky. For the first time, I was happy in the country.

Now we have a big yellow dog. Eric and I play with her every day. Someday I may have a pony. I write to my friends in the city. I miss them, but I am a country girl now!

Questions

Read and think.

1. Where did the family move?
2. Why did the girl say the new home looked scary?
3. What did Eric come up the walk with one day?
4. Why did the girl like her new home at last?

U·N·T·I·L
WE · BUILT · A · CABIN

When we lived in a city
(three flights up and down)
I never dreamed how many stars
could show above a town.

When we moved to a village
where lighted streets were few,
I thought I could see all the stars,
But, oh, I never knew—

Until we built a cabin
where hills are high and far,
I never knew how many
                many
                        stars there really are!

Aileen Fisher

WRITING ACTIVITY

WRITE A DESCRIPTIVE PARAGRAPH

Prewrite

Burly Bear liked his home on the water. The City Girl came to like her home in the country. A person may live in a big house. A person may live in a little house. A person may live in a strange house. Look at the pictures. What house might you like to live in?

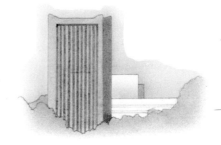

Make a picture of your house. Will it be huge or little? Will it be under water or up in the air?

Write

1. Look at the picture of your house.
2. Write a paragraph on your house on your paper.
3. This can be your first sentence.

    My house will be very special to me.
4. Write sentences that help people see your house in words.
5. Use your Glossary for help with words.

Revise

Read your paragraph. Did your sentences say what your house was like? Look at your picture. Does your paragraph say what is in your picture?

Read with your teacher.

1. Do your sentences begin with capital letters?
2. Do your sentences end with periods?

PREPARING FOR READING

Learning Vocabulary

Listen.

tree   sneakers   pony

Read.

1. You must <u>feed</u> and take <u>care</u> of a pet each day.
2. My <u>sister</u> says that I am a <u>babysitter</u> for my pet.
3. My sister and I take care of my pet <u>together</u>.

feed   care   sister
babysitter   together

Developing Background

Read and talk.

Your Babysitter

Your babysitter is a very special friend. A babysitter can be a girl or a boy, a brother or a sister. Grandma or Grandpa can be a babysitter, too. Your babysitter may read to you or play a game. Your babysitter may play ball or go swimming with you. A babysitter must like children. He or she must like to take care of children.

The Babysitter

Karen Young

My father works in a store. My mother teaches swimming. My big sister is away at school.

Jason works at my house. He's the babysitter. When I was little, my sister was my babysitter. Now, I am too big for a babysitter. So Jason and I take care of things together. Jason says I can be a big help.

I help Jason feed my brother, like my sister did me. We feed him together. You can see why a babysitter may need help.

I feed the pets every day. We have a
dog and a cat. I put water out for them,
too. I feed the pets so Jason can take
care of my brother.

Jason, my brother, and I go to the park together. My brother rides with Jason. I am so big that I can ride on my own. Jason and I play a game together. My brother is too little to play. We take him to see the little zoo in the park.

When we get home, Jason says that my brother and I can paint pictures. But my brother does not paint a picture. He paints his sneakers blue. They look so funny that I paint my sneakers green. Jason sees the sneakers, and he's not happy. He says that I am too big to do things like that. This is one time I wish I were little like my brother.

When I grow up, I will be a babysitter like Jason. I hope that I can take care of a boy like me. A boy like me is a big help to a babysitter!

Questions

Read and think.

1. Who is Jason?
2. What did the boy do to help Jason?
3. Where did Jason take the children?
4. Why does the boy want to be a babysitter, too?

PREPARING FOR READING

Learning Vocabulary

Listen.

tr<u>ee</u>   sn<u>ea</u>kers   pon<u>y</u>

Read.

1. My friends and I <u>scream</u> and jump up and down at a soccer game.

2. We eat <u>all</u> <u>kinds</u> of things, too.

3. We have a <u>good</u> time at the soccer game.

scream   all   kinds   good

Developing Background

Read and talk.

Soccer

We have a soccer team at my school. The coach is very good. She teaches the team to run fast and kick the ball. She teaches each boy and girl to move the ball up, down, and around with one foot. Now we know how to pass the ball and make points. She teaches all kinds of things to the team.

WHAT DO YOU WANT TO BE?

Linda Puner

Debbie, Lee, Carmen, and Daniel were on the school bus together. "Someday I want to drive a bus," said Carmen.

"I want to be a teacher," said Daniel.

"I want to be a dancer," said Lee. "What do you want to be, Debbie?"

"I don't know," said Debbie.

"All of my friends know what they want to be when they grow up," said Debbie to her mother that night. "What can I be?"

"You can be what you want," said Debbie's mother. "There are all kinds of things you can be."

"I don't want to be a teacher," said Debbie, "or a dancer. I don't want to drive a bus or a truck."

"You could fly a plane," said her mother, "or paint pictures."

"They are not the kinds of things I like to do," said Debbie. "I want to be something special, but I don't know what it is."

"I wish I could help you, Debbie," said her mother. "But you are the one who will know the kinds of things you like. Someday you will know what you want to be. You have time. I know now what I want to be."

"A mother, right?" asked Debbie.

"A mother and a soccer coach," said her mother.

"A soccer coach!" said Debbie. "You can't be a soccer coach!"

"Why not?" asked her mother. "I know the game. I played soccer when I was in school. Now your teacher says your school needs a new coach. I can be the new coach!"

Debbie liked to play soccer, but she did not want her mother to be the coach. "You will not like to come and work at my school," she said. "You will not like the children. They scream too much. You don't like it when children scream."

"Children should scream when they play soccer," said Debbie's mother. "It is all in the game."

"Then the children will not like you. You will scream at them too much," said Debbie.

"Why don't you want me to be your coach?" asked her mother.

"I am scared," said Debbie. "My school needs a good soccer coach. I am scared that you will not be a good soccer coach."

172

"I may be a good soccer coach, or I may not," said Debbie's mother. "I know I like soccer, so I will try to be a coach. Then we will see."

The next day Debbie, Lee, Carmen, and Daniel played soccer. Debbie's mother was there. "Keep your eye on the ball!" she called. "Take your turn! Come right up to the ball! Don't wait! Kick it now!" When Debbie's mother called "Time out!" all the players came up to Debbie.

"Carmen says the new coach is your mother," said Lee. "Is that true?" Then all the players spoke to Debbie at one time.

"What a good coach!" said Daniel. "What a good mother! I wish my mother could be a coach!"

"My mother played soccer when she was in school," said Debbie. "That is why she is a good coach now. I know now what I want to be when I grow up. I want to be a soccer coach, like my mother."

"Come on, team!" called the coach. "Time to play soccer!"

Questions

Read and think.

1. What did Debbie's mother want to be?
2. Why didn't Debbie want her mother to come to school?
3. What did the players say to Debbie?
4. What did Debbie want to be?

The Question

People always say to me
"What do you think you'd like to be
When you grow up?"
And I say, "Why,
I think I'd like to be the sky
Or be a plane or train or mouse
Or maybe a haunted house
Or maybe something furry, rough and wild . . .
Or maybe I will stay a child."

Karla Kuskin

175

PREPARING FOR READING

Learning Vocabulary

Listen.

miss	call
miss<u>ed</u>	call<u>ed</u>
miss<u>ing</u>	call<u>ing</u>

Read.

1. People were <u>laughing</u> and eating at the <u>picnic</u>.
2. There was too much <u>food</u> to eat.
3. There were too <u>many</u> of <u>us</u> to eat all the food.

laughing   picnic   food   many   us

Developing Background

Read and talk.

Picnic Spots

Where do you like to go on a picnic? I live in the city, so I like a picnic in the park. We take food and something to drink. Many people like to have a picnic in the country. I have friends who have a picnic at the bay and eat crab and flounder all day. For a picnic, all you need is food, people, and some sun.

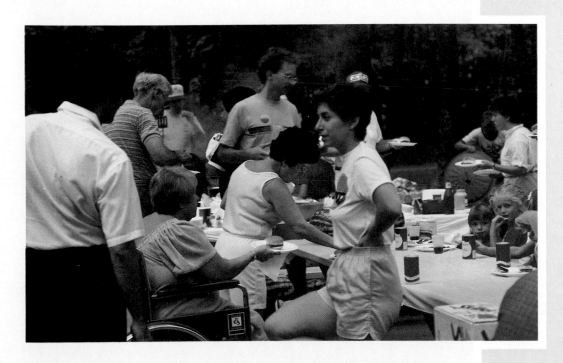

The Picnic

Barbara Kirk

My mother works with many people to make cars. The people she works with get together for a picnic. Mother and I go. She says that I can take pictures at the picnic. Then I can put many of the pictures in a book. I will write under all the pictures. She says that she may take the book to work to show her friends. I want her to do that. I hope that you like looking at the pictures of us at the picnic, too.

This is the huge park where the picnic was.

Many people liked the food.

There was so much food at the picnic! I liked eating the chicken and the fish. One man asked us to try eating some rabbit, so we did. There was too much to eat and drink. Mother said that eating all that food should make us sleep all day. There was not much food left.

We did eat and eat at the picnic, but
we played, too. Some of us played ball.
Ken's home run was something to see!
It was a very special game.

Go, Ken, go!

Come on, Ted!

You can see that this race was
pretty special, too. Running like this is
funny to see. People in the race were
laughing. People looking at the race
were laughing, too.

This is a picture of
my dog and me.

My friend Lisa
swam in the water.

Many people liked the swimming. Some of us were in a swimming race. People were calling to me and laughing when my dog came in first. He likes to swim.

Laughing, eating, swimming—we did it all. Mother says that it was a very special day for very special people.

Questions

Read and think.
1. What did the girl eat at the picnic?
2. What special race was very funny?
3. Who came in first in the swimming race?

PREPARING FOR READING

Learning Vocabulary

Listen.

a h<u>uge</u> bear

Read.

1. I <u>use</u> two <u>lights</u> to call my friends at night.
2. My friends are <u>twins</u> who look very much <u>alike</u>.
3. One night, I <u>saw</u> their lights go out, and I was scared.

use   lights   twins   alike   saw

Developing Background

Read and talk.

Your Eyes

Your eyes are very special to you. You should take good care of them. Some people use glasses to read but some do not. Some people must use glasses to drive a car or a truck. Some people do not need glasses at all. An eye doctor can help you take care of your eyes.

In *Who is Who?*, Chuckie and John go to see Dr. Hoover, the eye doctor. What will she do to help them?

185

WHO IS WHO?

Adair Sirota

Martin was running very fast up to Chuckie and John's house. "Do you want to play ball, John?" he called to Chuckie. "Come on, Chuckie," he called to John.

Chuckie and John were twins who looked very much alike. "You didn't get it right this time," said John, laughing.

Martin was laughing, too. "I didn't get a good look at you, John," he said. "I can't see who is Chuckie and who is John when I am running fast. Wait, I know! John, every day you should put on yellow sneakers. Chuckie, you should put on red sneakers. Then I will know who is who."

"We have new sneakers," said Chuckie.
"We can't paint them red or yellow. We
will try to come up with something to
help you, but not red and yellow sneakers."

Chuckie and John's mother came out
of the house. "Time to go," she said.

"We can't play ball with you now,
Martin," said John. "We have to go and
see the doctor. We will come to your
house when we get home."

When Dr. Hoover saw Chuckie and John, she said, "Twins! Let me see now, who is who?"

"This is John, Dr. Hoover," said his mother. "And this is Chuckie. Their teacher asked me to take John to an eye doctor, because he can't see his work at school."

"Will I have to get glasses?" asked John.

"We will see, John," said Dr. Hoover with a smile. "Now you may come with me."

Then Dr. Hoover said, "Sit down, John." She looked at each of his eyes. "You will use your right eye first." She turned down the lights. "Now, try to read the letters you see."

John saw the big letters. "**V, L, N, E**," he said. "I can't read the little letters."

"Now you will use your left eye to see the letters," said Dr. Hoover.

John could read the big letters, but he couldn't read the little letters. "My left eye and my right eye are alike," he said. "They both can see the big letters, but not the little letters."

Dr. Hoover turned the lights on. "Now you wait with your mother, John, and Chuckie can come in and see me," she said.

When he came in, Dr. Hoover asked Chuckie to sit down, too. She looked at his eyes. Then she turned the lights down. Chuckie called out the letters he could see with his right eye and then with his left eye. Then Dr. Hoover turned the lights on. "You may call your mother and John now," she said.

When they came in, Dr. Hoover said, "You have very good eyes, Chuckie. You have good eyes, too, John, but they need a little help. You will use glasses to help your eyes."

"You will look good in glasses, John," said his mother.

With Dr. Hoover's help, John picked the glasses he liked. He put them on for the first time. He looked at Chuckie and his mother. Then he looked at Dr. Hoover with a big smile. "Now I will see all my school work," he said.

"Now you will see all that you want to see," said Dr. Hoover.

When they were home, the twins
walked to Martin's house. Martin looked
at John. Then he looked at Chuckie.

"Now I know what doctor you saw!" he said. "You saw the eye doctor! John, that is good for you *and* for me. Now you and Chuckie do not look so much alike."

"You know what, Martin?" said John. "Now that I have my glasses, you and Chuckie do not look so much alike to me!"

Questions

Read and think.

1. Why did Chuckie and John look alike?
2. Why did the teacher say John should go to see an eye doctor?
3. Why was Martin happy that the doctor gave John glasses?

PREPARING FOR READING

Learning Vocabulary

Listen.

tree   sn<u>ea</u>kers   pon<u>y</u>

Read.

1. When I am <u>ready</u> for <u>bed</u>, I call Mother.

2. Then she will read a <u>story</u> to me.

3. I ask her to read it <u>over</u> and over.

4. <u>Later</u> she and I have something to eat.

ready   bed   story   over   later

Developing Background

Read and talk.

Sleeping Over

When you get big, you can have a friend sleep over at your house. I am Pilar and I want my friend, Rita, to sleep over. First I must call her. Then I must get her bed ready and go over what she and I might do. Later we will play, eat, and then it will be bedtime. I hope that we have a good time. What do you do when you have a friend sleep over?

PILAR AND RITA

Argentina Palacios

Pilar wanted to have a friend sleep over at her house. When she asked her mother, she said, "Later."

Pilar asked, "When is later?"

Her mother said, "Someday."

"When is someday?" asked Pilar.

Then her mother said, "When you are ready."

"I am ready now," said Pilar.

But her mother said, "Not now." Pilar gave up for a time.

Then one day Pilar asked, "May I have Rita come and sleep over for the night?"

Mother looked at her with a smile and said, "You may."

Pilar said, "What did you say?"

Mother said, "I said that you may have Rita sleep over. Go and call her now."

Pilar jumped up and down. "Hurray!" she screamed.

The big day came. Pilar was ready for Rita. At last Rita came. Pilar said to her, "My home is your home." Rita gave Pilar a big smile. Then Pilar said, "My mother says we can take a picnic to the park. Then we can go to the zoo."

At the park Pilar's mother said, "We will eat first. Then, when you are ready, we will go to the zoo."

Later, Pilar helped her mother pick up all their picnic things. "Now we are ready!" she said, so they left for the zoo.

"Look at the ostrich!" Pilar said. "He can kick!"

"I am not scared of a funny-looking ostrich," Rita said.

Then they saw a lion. "That lion could eat you," said Pilar, laughing.

Rita screamed, "He could not eat me! I am not scared of that lion!"

"We must go home," said Pilar's mother. "It will be bedtime by the time we get there."

They walked by the pet store. "I wish I could have a hamster," said Pilar.

"Not me," said Rita. "See that black cat? That is what I want. I am not scared of a black cat."

"Who said you were?" asked Pilar.

"Pilar," said her mother. "Do not say that to a friend."

At home Pilar's mother said, "Get ready for bed."

"May we have a bedtime story?" asked Pilar.

"We will each read a story," said Pilar's mother.

Pilar and Rita looked at stickers. They jumped up and down on the bed. Then Pilar's mother came in. "Time for bed," she said.

"You read first," said Pilar. So her mother read the story *Bedtime for Bears*. "You are next," said Pilar to Rita.

"I will read a scary story with a strange, huge turtle in it," said Rita. "I am not scared of a story like that."

Pilar read her story, *The Music Box*, last. Then it was time for bed.

The next day Pilar helped make the bed, but Rita did not help. Pilar picked up her sneakers and put them away, but Rita left her sneakers under the bed. "I have to feed my fish," said Pilar. "Do you want to help?"

But Rita did not want to help. "You must work all the time," she said.

Later in the day, Rita's mother came to get her. When she left, Pilar said to her mother, "I know something that Rita is scared of."

"What is that?" asked her mother with a smile.

"She is scared of work!" said Pilar.

Questions

Read and think.

1. What did Pilar want her mother to say she could do?
2. What did Pilar and Rita see at the zoo?
3. Why didn't Rita help Pilar with the work?

NOT
SCARED

The lion roars;
    The black bear growls;
The tiger snarls;
    The grey wolf howls.
But I'm not worried
    By their rages,
If they remain
    Inside their cages!

Ilo Orleans

PREPARING FOR READING

Learning Vocabulary

Listen.

miss	look
miss<u>ed</u>	look<u>ed</u>
miss<u>ing</u>	look<u>ing</u>

Read.

1. A little <u>duck</u> was <u>crying</u>.

2. He wanted to be <u>beautiful</u>.

3. Some ducks said that he was <u>ugly</u>.

4. He ran away <u>from</u> his <u>warm</u> home into the cold woods.

duck	crying	beautiful
ugly	from	warm

Developing Background

Read and talk.

Little Birds

When birds are little, they look ugly to some people. They can't fly or walk. The mother bird must keep them warm. They need to eat all the time. Their crying will keep both the mother and the father bird looking for food every day. Then at last, they are beautiful birds who will fly away to be on their own.

In the play, *The Ugly Duckling*, the storyteller and players act out a story about an ugly little duckling. Does the ugly duckling grow up to be a beautiful bird?

THE UGLY DUCKLING

Hans Christian Andersen
adapted by Karen Young

The Players

Mother Duck	**Chicken**	**Ugly Duckling**
Turtle	**Cat**	**Storyteller**
Brown Duck	**Swan**	

ACT ONE

Storyteller: One warm day, at a farm in the country, Mother Duck's new children came out of their eggs. Each duckling was small and yellow—all but the last one.

Brown Duck: You have some beautiful children there! But where did that ugly one come from?

Mother Duck: He is my duckling, too.

Turtle: He's not a duckling!

Brown Duck: (*laughing*) He must be an ostrich!

Mother Duck: He's not an ostrich. He can swim.

Turtle: (*laughing*) So can I. That does not make me a duckling.

Mother Duck: He can swim like a duck. He is one of my family. He was in the shell too long, that is all.

Storyteller: When the Ugly Duckling saw them laughing, he was sad.

Ugly Duckling: (*crying*) Why are they laughing at me? I will run away.

ACT TWO

Storyteller: The Ugly Duckling walked and walked. Much later, he walked up to a house in the woods. A woman, a cat, and a chicken were there. The cat and the chicken came out. The Ugly Duckling was crying.

Chicken: Why are you crying?

Ugly Duckling: I am crying because I don't know where to go. I know I am ugly, but may I live with you?

Cat: What? You must be something special to live with us.

Chicken: The woman gets eggs from me each day. Can she get eggs from you?

Ugly Duckling: She can't get eggs from me, but there are some things I can do.

Cat: I can use my claws to get a mouse. Can you?

212

Ugly Duckling: I don't have claws, but I can swim and dive in the water.

Chicken: What good is that? Don't try to make friends with us! Get out!

Ugly Duckling: They don't want me. Where can I go now?

ACT THREE

Storyteller: The Ugly Duckling came to the water. He was so sad. One day there was a scream in the sky.

Ugly Duckling: (*looking up*) What was that? Who screamed?

Storyteller: He saw some big, beautiful birds in the sky. They were swans.

Ugly Duckling: What beautiful birds! I don't know them, but I want to fly away with them. That is very strange. I wish I could fly.

Storyteller: The Ugly Duckling moved his wings, but he could not fly. The next day the air and the water turned very cold, and it was cold for a long time.

Ugly Duckling: I am so very cold, but I must keep swimming. I wish I were flying with the beautiful birds.

Storyteller: At last the air was warm.

Ugly Duckling: What a warm, beautiful day! I will try to fly now.

Storyteller: At last his wings worked. Flying high, he looked down. He saw the swans in the water.

Ugly Duckling: I am so ugly, but I will try to make friends. I know they will not want me.

Storyteller: Looking down, the Ugly Duckling swam up to the beautiful birds.

Ugly Duckling: I will look down, and they will not see that I am ugly.

Storyteller: Then he saw something strange in the water.

Ugly Duckling: Is that me I see in the water? My wings are long. I am beautiful!

Swan: Who are you, friend?

Ugly Duckling: I am the Ugly—wait, I am not ugly! I am like you!

Swan: Don't you know? You are a swan, and a beautiful one, too.

Ugly Duckling: I am a swan! I did not know I could be so happy when I was but an Ugly Duckling!

Questions

Read and think.

1. What did the Ugly Duckling do when he saw Turtle and Brown Duck laughing?
2. Who didn't want the Ugly Duckling to come and live with them?
3. Into what did the Ugly Duckling turn?

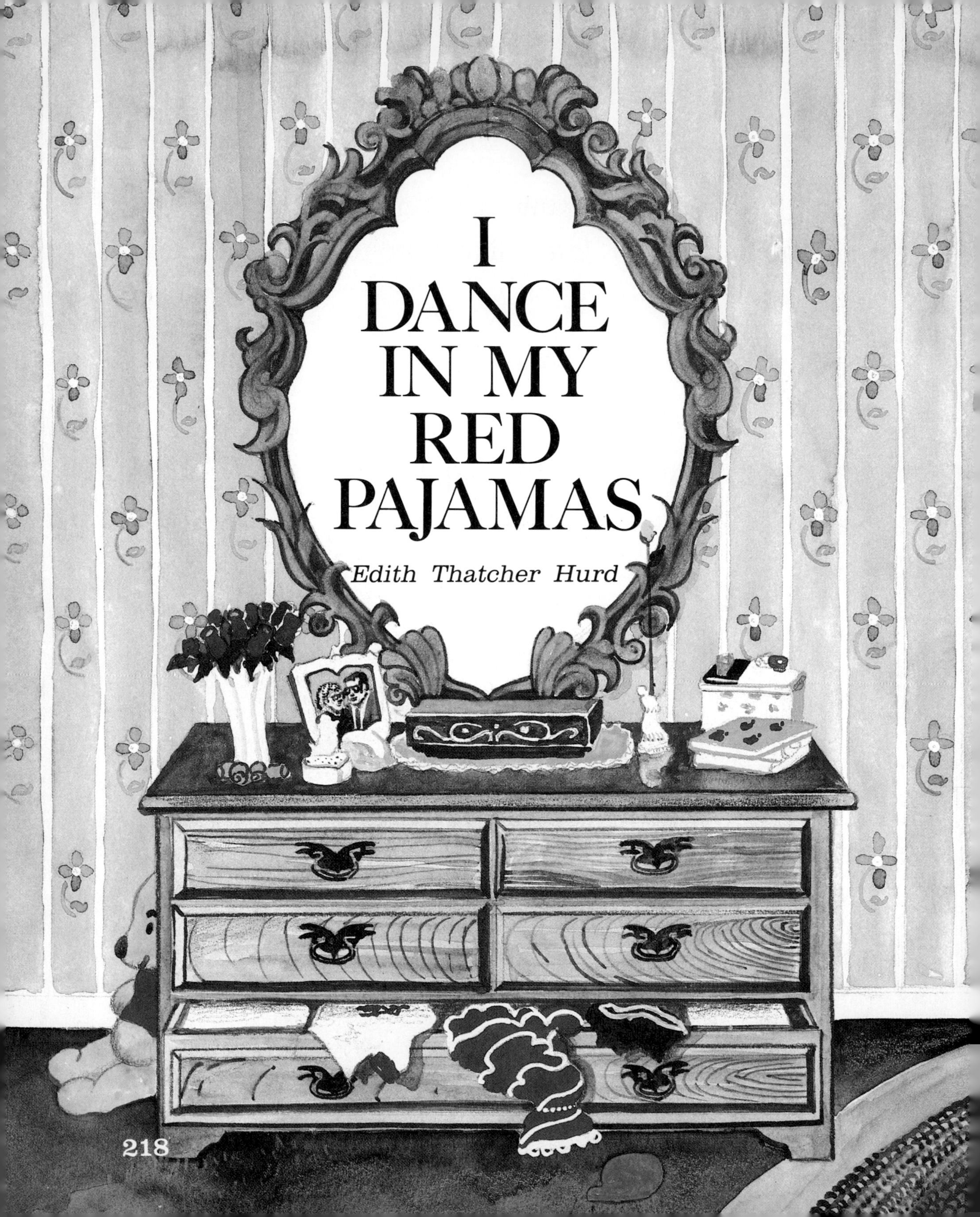

I
DANCE
IN MY
RED
PAJAMAS

Edith Thatcher Hurd

"Don't be too noisy, little Jenny," Mother says.

"Don't jump around and shout when you go to visit your Granny and your Grandpa," Father says.

I only smile and say, "Of course not."

My mother and my father think my Granny and my Grandpa are very old. They don't seem old to me, except my Granny's hair is white. Grandpa is just a little deaf, so he sometimes shouts at me.

When I go to their house, I take my red pajamas. I take my toothbrush. And I take my Lion, too.

I ring the bell, and when he sees me, Grandpa shouts, "Hey Granny, look who's here."

I shout right back, "It's me, Jenny. I've come to spend the night."

My Granny hugs me. My Grandpa is tall. He looks down and smiles at me.

When I go inside the house, Grandpa takes me by the hands. "Let's play the whirling game," he shouts.

I go whirling, whirling, whirling, and I'm singing, singing, singing.

"Oh, I'm busy, busy, busy,
getting dizzy, dizzy, dizzy."

When Grandpa puts me down, I wobble and I topple. I sing my whirling song.

"Oh, I'm busy, busy, busy,
getting dizzy, dizzy, dizzy."

221

"Come on, Jenny," Grandpa says. "I'm going to build a house outside, for Catarina." Catarina is Granny's big, fat, yellow cat.

"Nonsense," Granny says. "Why can't Catarina live in our house, the way she always has?"

"Because she wants to come in when she is out," grumbles Grandpa. "Then she wants to go out when she is in. Cats are like that."

"Nonsense," Granny says again. "Catarina will never live in a house by herself. Build a house for a mouse instead." Grandpa and I laugh, but we don't pay any attention.

Grandpa gets his hammer, and I get mine. We bang and we bang and we bang. But Granny is right. Catarina just yawns when we try to put her into the house that we built for her.

After we eat supper, I help with the dishes. Then I put on my red pajamas. I brush my teeth. I sit on the floor, with my Lion on one side and Catarina on the other. Grandpa makes a fire. We watch the fire spurting and spitting. We listen to the pops and the crackles. Granny begins to play the piano very softly. And I dance in my red pajamas.

When she plays louder, Grandpa and
I dance. We clap and we stomp as loud
as we can.

Granny calls,
"*Swing your partner and away
you go. Swing your partner
and a do-si-do.*"

Then Granny and Grandpa dance. They dance without any music, just humming the tune to each other. When they are through, Grandpa says, "That's the way Granny and I used to dance on soft summer nights long ago."

I had never thought about Granny and Grandpa dancing together. But I am too sleepy to say anything more. So Grandpa picks me up piggyback, and takes me upstairs. Granny tucks me into my bed. We give each other hugs and Lion, too. "Good night, Granny," I say.

"Good night, Jenny," she says.

But Grandpa says, "Oh, what a beautiful, lovely, noisy day."

Glossary

A

act   Pilar played a bear in the first <u>act</u> of the play.

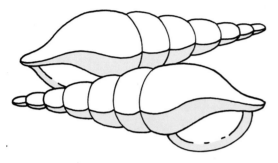

a · like   Nan looked for shells that were <u>alike</u>.

all   <u>All</u> the children in school came to the play.

a · round   Mr. Park put a rope <u>around</u> the box.

a · way   Jeff may go <u>away</u> to live in a big house.

B

ba · by · sit · ter   The <u>babysitter</u> will take care of Emily when her mother is at work.

bal · let   The <u>ballet</u> teacher will show the children each step.

bas · ket · ball   Lisa likes to play <u>basketball</u> with her friends.

beau · ti · ful   When the sun came up, the sky looked <u>beautiful</u>.

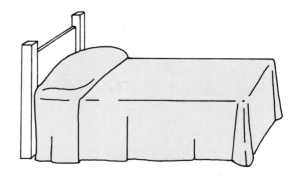

bed   The little boy will go to sleep when he gets in his <u>bed</u>.

broth·er   Jennifer walks to school with her <u>brother</u>.

by   The boy sits <u>by</u> the tree.

C

care   Kate will feed, water, and <u>care</u> for her new pet kitten.

club   Don will show his shell collection at the hobby <u>club</u>.

coach   The basketball <u>coach</u> teaches the team to make shots.

col·lec·tion   Mark and Pam make a <u>collection</u> of shells for a hobby.

crow   A <u>crow</u> is a bird.

cry·ing   The little girl was <u>crying</u> because she lost her cat.

D

dance   Jonathan and Karen will <u>dance</u> in the play.

danc·er   The <u>dancer</u> turned very fast on one foot.

doc·tor   The <u>doctor</u> will know if Sue needs glasses.

drib·ble   Kim can <u>dribble</u> the ball when she is running.

drink   The dog likes a <u>drink</u> of water when the air is hot.

drove   Mother <u>drove</u> the children to school in the car.

drum   You can make a drum with a box or a can.

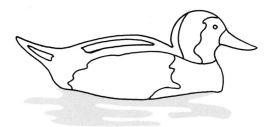

duck   The duck walked to the water and swam away.

duck·ling   The mother duck had one little duckling.

E

eve·ry   Mr. Miller runs every day.

eye   The flying ball gave Eric a black eye.

F

fam·i·ly   There are three people in Paco's family.

feed   Rita and Bob feed their pet turtle every day.

float   Tami can swim and she can float.

food   What kinds of food do you like to eat?

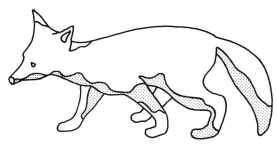

fox   A fox looks something like a dog.

from   The family drove from the city to the country.

G

gave   Mother and Father gave a pony to Kim.

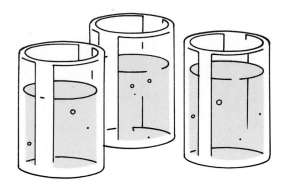

glass·es   Mother asked Mabel to put water in the <u>glasses</u>.

good   The coach said that the team played a <u>good</u> game.

grand·ma   <u>Grandma</u> likes to read to the children.

grand·pa   <u>Grandpa</u> takes Rita fishing with him.

H

ham·ster   Bart likes his pet <u>hamster</u>.

her   Carmen can show the children <u>her</u> pictures.

high   The plane is flying very <u>high</u> in the sky.

his   Ted put down <u>his</u> book.

hob·by   Some people like to paint for a <u>hobby</u>.

hoop   Emily can put the ball in the <u>hoop</u> for her team.

hur·ray   Cathy calls "<u>hurray</u>!" when the team gets points.

I

in·stru·ment   What <u>instrument</u> can you play to make music?

K

keep   Kirk and Linda <u>keep</u> looking for the lost kitten.

kinds   A pet store will have all <u>kinds</u> of dogs.

know   Rosa and Tami <u>know</u> where the pet store is.

lat·er   First the girls will play soccer, then <u>later</u> they will go swimming.

laugh·ing   Mother was <u>laughing</u> at the funny show.

left   Anne <u>left</u> school and walked home.

life·sav·ing   The swimming coach teaches the children <u>lifesaving</u>.

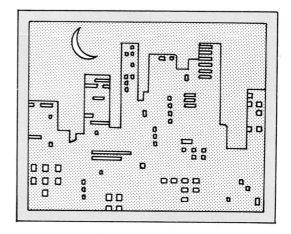

lights   Amanda likes the <u>lights</u> of the city at night.

lost   "Have you seen my <u>lost</u> dog?" asked the little boy.

M

man·y   There are <u>many</u> people in the city.

might   Nan <u>might</u> be first in the race because she runs very fast.

move   Ben will <u>move</u> to a house in the city.

mu·sic   Elena and Carmen like to dance to <u>music</u>.

N

nails   Muffy will need <u>nails</u> to make a house for the bird.

need   Pam and Rosa <u>need</u> sneakers for running.

new   Pip will make <u>new</u> friends in the country.

next   Jenny will sit <u>next</u> to Fred.

O

pic·nic   The family will eat, drink, and swim at their <u>picnic</u> in the park.

o·ver   Mark asked Eric to come <u>over</u> to his house to play.

own   Each bird flew to its <u>own</u> home.

P

pitch·er   There was water in the <u>pitcher</u>.

play·ers   There are five <u>players</u> on a basketball team.

pass   When Jane gets the ball, she will <u>pass</u> it to Sue.

points   Katie helps her team make <u>points</u> in the basketball game.

pool   Jan and Karen go to the swimming <u>pool</u> every day.

R

rab·bit   Jack wanted to have a <u>rabbit</u> for a pet.

race   Paco runs in the <u>race</u> with his friends.

read·y   The family is <u>ready</u> to go on a picnic.

right   The boy on your <u>right</u> is Sam.

rocks   The children pick up the pretty <u>rocks</u> that they see.

S

sang   The bird <u>sang</u> when the sun came up.

saw   When David looked up, he <u>saw</u> his friend Ted.

scared   The little kitten was <u>scared</u> of the big dog.

scream   The children <u>scream</u> when the players on their team make points.

shots   Jeff works on his <u>shots</u> to put the ball in the hoop.

sis·ter   Mother asked Tim to take care of his little <u>sister</u>.

skip   To <u>skip</u>, you must jump on one foot.

small   The little girl was too <u>small</u> to run in the race.

smile   The funny bears make the boy smile.

snap   You can snap two shells to make music.

sneak·ers   Jane and Tim have on sneakers when they play basketball.

soc·cer   Soccer is a team game.

spe·cial   Carmen was a special friend of Sam.

spread   The team spread out to play the game.

step   The children did each dance step with the teacher.

stick·ers   Maria put her stickers in a book.

store   The woman looked for apples in the store.

sto·ry   The children want their mother to read them a story when they go to bed.

sto·ry·tell·er   The storyteller will make up a new story for the children.

strange   It is strange to see a bear dance.

swam   David swam in the warm water of the bay.

swan   A swan is a beautiful bird.

swim·ming   The children like to go swimming when it is hot.

T

tap   The teacher will <u>tap</u> her foot in time to the music.

team   Charlene is on the ball <u>team</u> for her school.

their   The children like <u>their</u> teacher.

there   <u>There</u> was a letter for each of the children.

things   What <u>things</u> do you need to paint a picture?

thirst·y   Rosa is very <u>thirsty</u> so she will drink the water.

to·geth·er   Lisa and her brother walk to school <u>together</u>.

tree   The apples on the <u>tree</u> are big and red.

trick   Jack can do a special <u>trick</u> to make his dog come home.

try   The children <u>try</u> to dance in time to the music.

turn   The children <u>turn</u> to see José race by on his pony.

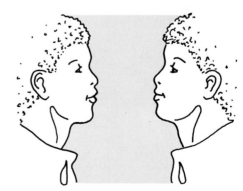

twins   Some <u>twins</u> look alike, but some do not.

237

u

ug·ly   Pamela said, "My picture is not pretty. It is <u>ugly</u>."

us   When Ben and I left school, Grandpa picked <u>us</u> up.

use   The girls will <u>use</u> a can to make a drum.

w

wait   Jim and Sally <u>wait</u> for the bus to take them to school.

want   Bart and Paco <u>want</u> to go to the zoo.

warm   The dog was <u>warm</u> and happy when it played in the sun.

whoosh   The wind blew with a huge "<u>whoosh!</u>"

wings   A bird and an airplane both have <u>wings</u>.